A Brief Guide to Historic Bray

A Stroll Around the Village

All profits from the sale of this book will be donated to The Friends of St Michael's, Bray

Published in the United Kingdom by
Chris Graham
7 Bray Close
Bray, Maidenhead
Berkshire
SL6 2BL

chris.graham@brayclose.com

Compiled and edited by Julie Graham
Content copyright © Julie Graham, 2022

All rights reserved. No portion of this book may be reproduced, stored in a retrieval system or transmitted at any time or by any means mechanical, electronic, photocopying, recording or otherwise, without the prior, written permission of the publisher.

The right of Chris Graham to be identified as the publisher of this work has been asserted by him in accordance with the Copyright, Designs and Patent Act 1988.

Printed by Lulu
First published in November 2022

Layout and Design by Julie Graham

ISBN 978-0-9561771-1-7

A Stroll Around the Historic Village of Bray

Section 1 : Introduction

Section 2 : Bray Village

Section 3 : Old Mill Lane and Monkey Island

Section 4 : Natural Bray

Section 5 : Early History

Section 6 : Acknowledgements

SECTION 1 : INTRODUCTION

Welcome to the historic village of Bray. It is set within the Civil Parish of Bray which also contains the villages of Holyport[1], Fifield and Oakley Green. The Parochial Parish of Bray, which extends to the A4 at Maidenhead in one direction, and to Holyport and Fifield in the other, has St Michael's Church at its heart. This guide began life several years ago as a Heritage Trail. Following interest from the Maidenhead Archaeological and History Society, it has now been expanded. Whilst there are far more detailed books written about Bray, the purpose of this guide is to provide an overview as you walk around with some background stories and information included.

Extract from The Topographical Map of Berkshire by John Rocque, dated 1761, showing Bray village, Bray Mead *(now Old Mill Lane, Bray Bank & River Gardens)*, Duke of Marlborough Island *(now Monkey Island)* and Hollyport.

---

[1] Holyport, spelt Hollyport on John Roque's Topographical Map of Berkshire dated 1761. It is still pronounced as if the first part was written "Holly". The name Bray Mead (meadow) also appears on the same map to describe the land to the west of the Thames near Bray.

The 1848 Post Office (PO) Directory describes Bray as a *"small but healthy Village"*. This guide takes you on a stroll around the centre of the village. Section 2 provides some background on the history along with notes on people who have lived and worked here, and the organisations. The information contained within has been gleaned from a variety of sources – stories from local residents, church and Parish booklets, books written about Bray, old records and newspaper articles. One resident has an amazing collection of old post cards, a few of which are included. If you compare then and now, not a lot has changed.

The small paintings by Liz Cooper come from a map, commissioned by the author, for Queen Elizabeth II's Diamond Jubilee in 2012 called Royal Heritage in the Parish of Bray, which identified all the royal connections within the Parish.

Should you wish to walk beyond the village centre, Section 3 includes several of the buildings within the vicinity. Section 4, Natural Bray, suggests walks and explores a little of the wildlife in the area whilst Section 5 explains the history of early Bray.

The centre of the village of Bray has been given the status of "Conservation Area" meaning that it has buildings of *"special architectural or historic interest, the character or appearance of which it is desirable to preserve or enhance".*[2] (see plan) There are 26 listed buildings and structures within the village of Bray with a further 2 in the surrounding area to which reference is made.[3]

---

[2] Special interest in a Conservation Area can be the result of a number of characteristics, such as an historic street pattern, traditional building styles, one or more listed buildings or possibly an association with an historic event or figure, or a local industry or trade. The practical implications mean that if people living in Bray want to undertake any building work or changes to their property, they need to seek advice.

[3] A listed building, structure (eg a monument), or site (eg a battlefield or shipwreck), has been placed on one of the three statutory lists, the main purpose of which is to preserve our heritage and the most important historic places. In this country the lists are maintained by Historic England with similar organisations in Wales, Scotland and Northern Ireland.

CATEGORIES OF LISTED BUILDINGS

- Grade I buildings are of exceptional interest
- Grade II* buildings are particularly important and of more than special interest
- Grade II buildings are nationally important and of special interest

The next section deals with specific sites within Bray Village. Enjoy your walk!

An aerial view of Bray with St Michael's Church in the centre and the River Thames behind. The white building between the church and the river is the old Vicarage

All proceeds from the sale of this guide will be donated to The Friends of St Michael's who raise funds to maintain the historic fabric of the church building and churchyard.

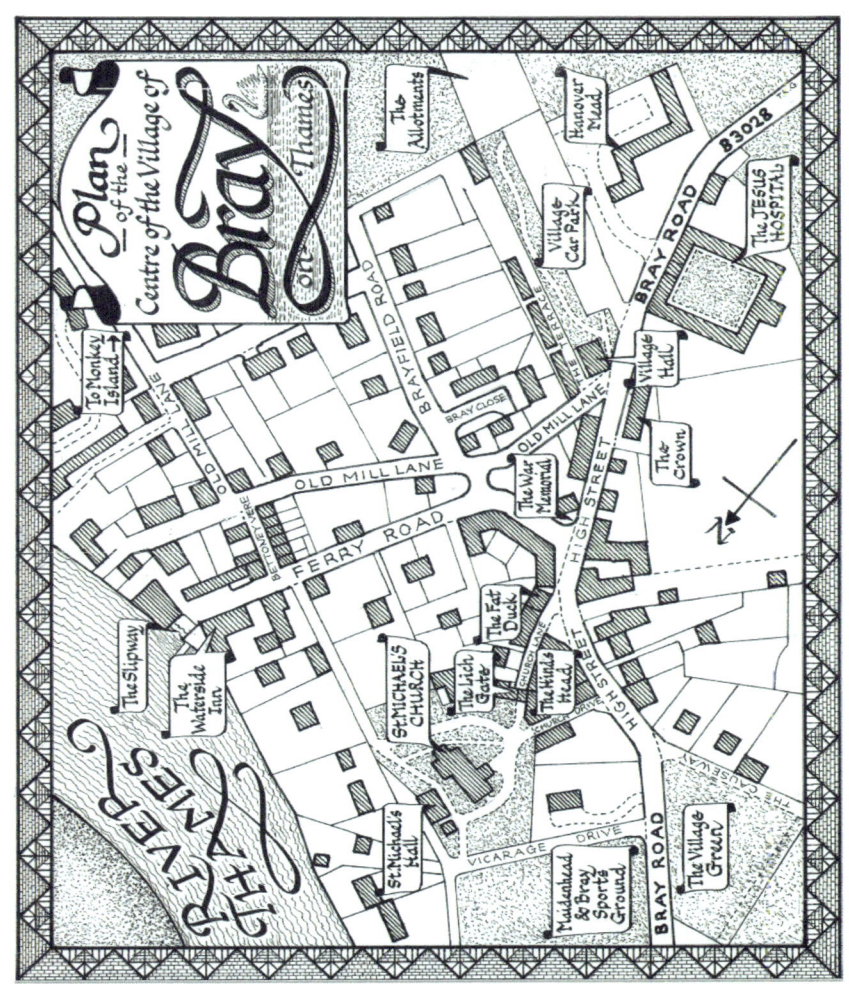

plan of Bray Village drawn by Trevor Gould

SECTION 2 : BRAY VILLAGE

Bray was a royal manor, belonging to the ancient demesne of the Crown – a feudal term meaning that the land was attached to a manor and was retained by the owner for their personal use. It also formed part of the "liberty" of Windsor Forest.[4] In medieval times, although owned by the King, Bray formed part of the Queen's Dowry and she became Patron of the Church. Bray has also been owned variously by the Augustinian Abbey of Cirencester; it was returned to the Crown following Henry VIII's Dissolution of the Monasteries (1536-1540); then to the Bishop of Oxford around 1550. During the period of the Commonwealth (1649-1660) the manor was taken over by the Parliamentary Commissioners but later restored to the Crown. Charles II finally returned Bray to the Bishop of Oxford in whose Diocese it remains.

In the 1854 PO Directory, it states the living was a vicarage, value £500 with 400 acres of glebe land – meaning the land was owned by the Diocese and the Vicar received his income through money and food raised from this land. The old Vicarage lies behind the church and has the remains of a Tudor fireplace, with the modern Vicarage to the right. Although very much a 1950's style building, the setting is splendid with the garden leading down to the river; summer events include cream teas and Jazz on the Lawn.

The following items take you on a tour of the Conservation Area of Bray. In particular, the listed buildings and monuments mentioned in the introduction are identified and brief notes provided. The Roman numbers in brackets show the listing grade.

1. **St Michael's Church (II*)**

Start with St Michael's Church as it is easy to find. You may be lucky and find the church open and someone inside who can point

---

[4] The "liberty" of Windsor Forest – another term from the medieval period allowing someone to act in community affairs and to exert influence on one's fellows without interference from the government.

out the key features. Leaflets providing more detailed information are available on the table.

The present church was built around 1293 by Queen Margaret, the second wife of Edward I, near an ancient crossing of the Thames. It replaced a much older Saxon building which was probably situated about a mile away although no evidence remains. The name Reinbald, and the date 1081, which is the first on the board citing the Vicars of Bray, will come from this earlier period.

Being a royal foundation meant that the church was larger and therefore more expensive to build than would be expected relative to the size of population; local parishioners complained at the cost.

The tower, which is made of flint and clunch (a type of hard chalk), was built c1400 and, nowadays, contains a ring of 8 bells, the earliest dating from 1612. A full peal was rung to celebrate Victory in Europe on Wednesday 8th May 1945 at the end of World War II. Robert "Bobby" Howes, one of the village's long-standing and more elderly residents, was a bellringer at the time and recalls it took 3 hours 10 minutes. There is a board and photograph in the ringing chamber which commemorates this event. Bobby is third from the right, next to the board.

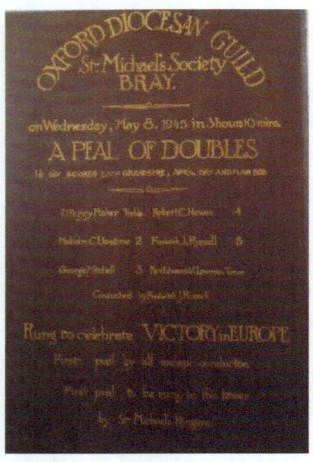 

The tower clock was installed in 1840. The stone benches in the porch are worn, showing where village meetings were once held. Notice the two wooden benches situated either side of the external gates. The one on the left is engraved *"Geoffrey G Messum Boats at Bray for 50 years".* More about him later.

When St Michael's was first built, the walls were brightly painted with Bible stories and the lives of saints; a means of informing people who could not read and write. There were no fixed seats other than those let into the walls which were for the use of the frail and elderly. The rest of the congregation walked about, chattering, until reminded by the ringing of the Sanctus-bell as to why they were there. Later, tiered box pews were fitted, parallel to the walls and rented out to local families. In 1857-62, during a major reconstruction project instigated by the then vicar, the **Reverend James Austen-Leigh,** nephew of author Jane Austen, pews were installed which are still in use today. In the 1887 Kelly's Directory, it states there were *"1200 sittings, all free".* This must have been quite squashed as nowadays the capacity is around 450.

The 1871 Census shows that the Rev Austen-Leigh was still living in the Vicarage and serving as Vicar of Bray. His four unmarried sons were in their 20s and 30s, one being a Clerk in the House of Commons, the next a Curate of Bray, the third an Assistant Master at Eton and a Fellow of King's College, Cambridge, and the youngest, a Clerk in the House of Lords and also a Fellow of King's

College, Cambridge. Apparently all four brothers were first class cricketers.

If you are able to see inside, look out for the following:

the Royal Arms of James I dated 1604 – these were taken down by parishioners and hidden during the Commonwealth. The Arms were replaced after the Restoration and can be seen on the screen to the right of the chancel. The fact that they survived, and were not destroyed, makes them unusual.

- the 28 heads which were carved on to the capitals of the pillars during the reconstruction project, reproducing the original medieval villagers, plus some Victorian additions; the Rev Austin-Leigh can be seen looking over your shoulder next to the left hand pulpit;

- the Gothic font which was purchased in 1647 for £3.15s.9d;

- the alabaster monument to William Goddard (died 1609), founder of Jesus Hospital, to the left of the main altar;

11

- brass memorials set into the walls;
- the altar was moved to the nave's first bay in 1968 and a new sanctuary area created, thus bringing the focal point of a service nearer to the congregation.

There are two versions of a story linked to the infamous **Vicar of Bray**. He was an incumbent of this parish who switched his allegiance from Papist to Protestant depending who was on the throne and therefore which religion was favoured. Reputedly, he had witnessed martyrs burned in Windsor and did not wish to be seen supporting the "wrong side".

One version links the Vicar (Symon Aleyn) to the reigns of Henry VIII, Edward VI, Mary and finally Elizabeth, even though there was more than one Vicar during this period, whilst the ballad of The Vicar of Bray refers to then Vicar, Francis Carswell, and to Charles II, James II, Mary and William III, Anne and finally George I. Basically, he kept changing sides depending who was king or queen and their preferred faiths! Either way, the Vicar concerned succeeded in maintaining his principles of living and dying the Vicar of Bray, as the chorus states:

If you go into the Hinds Head, there is a reference to this poem inscribed on the mantle over the fireplace.

Walking round the outside of the church, you may be able to spot, what is thought to be, a cannon ball embedded in the south wall near the small door to the right of the porch. It looks like a piece of rusty metal compared to the grey flintstones. Legend has it that it was shot during the Civil War, although there is no evidence to prove this.

During the Civil War, leading up to the Commonwealth Period, Windsor Castle served as a garrison for members of the Earl of Essex's Parliamentary army from 1642-1645 occupying both a defensive and strategic position.[5] On the 7th November 1642, Windsor was attacked by Prince Rupert, on behalf of the Royalists and Charles I, and local residents had to seek refuge in the Forest of Windsor.

Windsor Castle was also used as a prison with the wealthy being able to pay for better accommodation. Charles I was imprisoned here in 1648, under "house arrest", before being taken to London where he was tried and condemned to death.

The Windsor Garrison Accounts for this period (1642-1645) still exist. Windsor was used as a supply base for not only the castle and town, but also the middle Thames Valley, South West England and the South Midlands. The River Thames, running through Bray, was used for transporting goods as far as Henley where it became

---

[5] With thanks to Elias Kupfermann, a local historian, who gave a talk entitled Windsor Castle in the Civil War to the Maidenhead Archaeological and History Society, and who has allowed me to use this background information and slide.

rapids and roads were then used. Resources were collected and paid for on a parish-by-parish basis, including the Bray Hundred.[6] This extract shows that Bray provided oats, hay and money.

It is speculated that its proximity to the River Thames meant that Bray became an additional burial site for the victims of the Plague in 1665, the number of dead having overwhelmed the London churchyards.

2. Tombstones (II)

Continue walking round the churchyard. The instructions for finding these tombstones are not entirely clear but it is interesting to look around all the same.

- Adams chest tomb approximately 7 metres north of the middle aisle of the church;
- group of 4 chest tombs, approximately 6 metres north-east of north chapel;
- group of 5 gravestones, approximately 4 metres south-east of south chapel.

3. St Michael's Hall (II), previously known as The Old Schoolroom

This is situated around the back of the church. A new toilet block has been built alongside.

---

[6] A Hundred was a unit of English Local Government and taxation which continued until the 19th century. It was thought originally to consist of 100 "hides" – a unit of land which supported a peasant family. (source = Encyclopedia Britannica)

Originally built as a **"Chauntry Chapel of the Blessed Virgin Mary"** c1293, probably with the purpose of praying for the soul of Edward I's first wife, Queen Eleanor. She had been granted the land around Bray, which was used for farming. It ceased to be a chapel in the sixteenth century. A piscina (a stone basin which was used for draining water used in the Mass) is still visible in the east end where the Chauntry altar would have been.

It is suggested the building was then used to dry and store fishermen's nets from hooks in the ceiling.

In 1683, the building became a school for 20 poor boys of the Parish and the east end enclosed to make a cottage for the master. Ernie Clinch, the last tenant, left in 1959 – he had 3 children and, as Sexton, was responsible for the heating in the church, including stoking the boilers. During the 1940s-50s the hall was used by the **BBC – Bray Boxing Club**. It was run by Fred Johnson, landlord of the Ringers pub. A local resident, Paul Tillion of Sunflower Cottages, recalls fights with other local clubs from Windsor, Maidenhead & St Luke's Boys' School which were held in Bray Village Hall where a full-sized boxing ring was assembled. The whole of the St Michael's Hall is now used by the church.

Look out for: on the outside south wall to the left of the entrance, the old stone with a carving of an animal, possibly a dog or leashed hound, which is thought may have come from the original Saxon church.

15

To the left of St Michael's Hall used to be **The Timber Engine House** where the village **Fire Engine** was kept, although to begin with, it was placed in the church itself. A Newsham ten-man engine was acquired by the Parish in 1737, the gift of the Right Honourable Anne, Lady Coleraine of Canon Hill.

The Church Warden's accounts (1760-1803) show that different men were paid 2 guineas (£2 2shillings) to keep the engine in *"good and useful repair"*. One of these, Mr Pattison, *"is to instruct 6 young persons to learn the art of playing the said Engine who shall live in the Town of Bray and that the engine is not taken out of the Church without the said Mr Pattison's knowledge unless it be on cases of emergency"*.

The Fire Engine continued to be maintained by the church during the 19th century, then in May 1900 it was agreed that the newly appointed Bray Parish Council should take charge of it. For a while it resided in The Eagle at Holyport (now The Belgian Arms) before being moved back to Bray in 1903. The Fire Brigade Act of 1938 removed the power from the Parish Councils and by the end of that year *"Maidenhead Fire Brigade will undertake Fire Extinction Services in the Parish of Bray"*. Bobby Howes remembers that his grandfather used to work on the fire engine.

What do you do with an old Fire Engine? It has been in store at a local museum and then on display at a College of Fire Fighters for several decades but the current plan is for the Engine to return to

Maidenhead where it is hoped there will be a permanent home found at the new Heritage Centre.

As you stand facing the porch, there is a brick wall to your left with Chauntry House behind. A better view can be had from the cricket club, further on.

4. Chauntry House (II)

The current Georgian house dates from 1753 and was probably built as a workhouse, almshouse & jail, some evidence for which is still visible in the basement. Luke Over & Chris Tyrrell in their book "The Royal Hundred of Bray" quote from a report dated 1906 describing two cells in the cellars which had *"gratings and spiked iron doors"*. In 1815 the population in the workhouse was 55. By 1861 the house was privately owned and rebuilt accordingly.
In the 1860s two sisters, **Mary and Anne Wilson**, moved into Chauntry House. Their father, William Wilson, had owned a successful linen-drapers in Covent Garden, London. In 1847 Mary and Anne, with their brother John, spent 10 months travelling around Belgium, Germany, Italy and Switzerland. Mary kept a diary while Anne painted many illustrations of the places they visited. The illustrated journal was later published.[7] Mary and Anne never married, preferring to remain independent. They moved several times before settling in Bray where Mary died in 1873. The 1881 Census shows Anne Sa(u)nders Wilson, aged 74, born in Covent Garden, living in "Chantry" House with a Visitor staying and 4 servants – a Cook, Parlour Maid, House Maid and Coachman. She died in 1883, leaving a personal estate of £34,409 0s 6d (nearly £3m in today's money).

Lady Smith, who owned Chauntry House in the 1930s, opened it up every Ascension Day and put on a party for the children from **Braywick School** in Hibbert Road (now rebuilt as Braywick Court School). Bobby Howes, who was 6 at the time, remembers that, although the school was closed for the day, the children still had to

---

[7] A European Journal – Two Sisters Abroad in 1847: Mary Wilson with illustrations by Anne Wilson

attend the party but they didn't mind as there were treats such as games and ice cream.

There were several other inhabitants before the house was converted into flats in 1950. In 1965 some rooms were used as an antiques showroom, with the house becoming a hotel restaurant in the 1970s. It is now once again a private residence.

Walk away from the church, down Church Drive. Ahead of you is:
Aleyn House (no 1 The High Street). At the end of the nineteenth century, this used to be the local dairy. Milk was sold here by the **Woodhouse family**. The cows were led through the village each day from the fields on which now stands Hanover Mead, opposite Jesus Hospital. The wisteria, which still grows across the back of the house, was planted for one son, **William Edward Basil Woodhouse**, whose name is inscribed on the War Memorial having served as a Company Serjeant Major with the 8th Battalion of the Royal Berkshire Regiment during the First World War. He was killed 24th February 1917 on the Western Front at Assevilliers. The 1911 Census showed him married, with a young child, and working as Sexton at Bray Church. The same census has his mother, Emily Eliza Woodhouse as Dairywoman, assisted by her daughter, Ivy Cecile.

Return to the churchyard towards the Lich Gate with St Michael's Cottage to the left; through the Lich Gate and into Church Lane.

5. St Michael's Cottage and Iron Railings (II); Lich Gate dated 1448 (II*)

Lich or "lych" is an old English or Saxon word meaning corpse; in the Middle Ages when bodies were buried in shrouds rather than coffins, the dead were carried to the Lich Gate, placed on a bier and the priest carried out the first part of the funeral service before entering the church.

It is thought that the Chantry priest may have lived above the Lich Gate, before the buildings were sold or rented as private homes. Another suggestion is that the corner window was used as a look-out against body snatchers who were intent on digging up newly

> *Look out for:* the date 1448
> 1448 carved in Arabic numerals on the timber post & in a timber under the arch, next to the wrought iron gate. The "loop" representing the number 4, signifies half the number 8.

dug graves in order to steal and sell the bodies for medical and anatomical research. Stealing the bodies was not actually illegal although dissecting them was. The law changed with the 1832 Anatomy Act allowing physicians, surgeons and medical students to legally dissect donated bodies, that is, unclaimed bodies from institutions such as prisons, hospitals and workhouses.

The postmark on the back of the card is dated July 1906

At one stage, the Lich Gate was apparently a beer house known as **"The Six Bells"**, since there were 6 bells in the church tower at the time. In 1839 the buildings surrounding the Lich Gate were bought by the Revd Walter Levett and the present apartments built, although much restored in the 1960s. In 1853, the Revd Levett established a charitable Trust which provides an almshouse, consisting of a cottage and a garden. This Charity of the Rev Walter Levett is also named Bray Lich Gate Trust.

Walk down Church Lane, originally known as St Thomas's Street. The cottages mentioned below refer to those which are listed.

Church Lane contains some of the oldest cottages in Bray, likely to be around the 15th century. Standing with the Lich Gate behind you, those on the right were once called Church Cottages and the ones on the left, Lych Cottages.

6. Lych Gate Cottage (II); Yew Tree Cottage (II); Dormer Cottage (II); No 3 Church Lane (II)

Before the cottages were modernised, there was a yard behind with a communal wash-copper and the residents were allotted days when they could use it. Water was drawn from a nearby well. Christmas Cottage, which has been fitted in between Yew Tree Cottage and Dormer Cottage, is a "new" addition. Hinds Head Cottage has now been absorbed into the Hinds Head.

Church Lane looking towards the High Street with the Hinds Head on the right

7. Hinds Head Cottage (II) and Hinds Head Hotel (II)

The current building is probably a late 15th century timber framed hall house before being divided into two cottages. Its original purpose is open to speculation – it may have been a hospice linked to the Abbey of Cirencester, one time owner of Bray Church, or possibly a royal hunting lodge. The right-hand cottage became a small inn, until, in 1928 Kitty Henry (also known as **"Champagne Kitty"** because of her high standards) bought the inn and adjoining cottage. A dining room was built to the left and in 1932 she also acquired the cottage behind (Hinds Head Cottage) in Church Lane. An annual sight was the meet of hounds outside the Hinds Hind on Boxing Day.

The Hinds Head became famous amongst royalty and film stars. On 23rd April 1963, the day before Princess Alexandra's wedding to Angus Ogilvy, the Queen and Prince Philip entertained royal guests for lunch enjoying saddle of lamb followed by treacle tart.

In 1955, the **Rolls-Royce Enthusiasts' Club** was launched at the Hinds Head. 1955 also marked the launch of the Rolls-Royce Silver Cloud and Bentley S Series motor cars. Sixty years later a rally of more than 60 cars took place on the Village Green with Rolls-Royces and Bentleys coming from around the UK and Europe. They made quite a sight as they processed through the village.

8. Nos 1 and 2 Oldfield View (II); The Fat Duck (II) (formerly The Ringers Public House)

It is speculated that the name **Oldfield View** comes from the fact that Oldfield, the name given to the Common Land now known as the Village Green, could be seen from the cottages. In 1819, 16 householders had access to the "Bray Common Allotment" where they were allowed to graze one cow per person.

The **Fat Duck** was originally built as a cottage in the 16th century with evidence of wattle and daub being discovered during restoration work in the 1960s. The earliest known deed dates from 1744. At some point, it became a Beer House. There is mention given of the name **Ringers** in the 1871 Census with William Moore as Publican. The same person is described as Beer-house Keeper in the 1861 Census but the name of the inn is not given. In 1896, it was leased to John Fuller the Brewer.

Reference has already been made to one of the landlords, Fred Johnson, who ran the Ringers with his wife, Jean, in the 1940s-50s, as well as overseeing the Bray Boxing Club. It retained the name Ringers, until **Heston Blumenthal** took over the building in 1995 and the now world-famous restaurant, **The Fat Duck,** was born.

Walk along the High Street towards the War Memorial taking a sideways glance at Ferry End built in 1904 by T.J. Rigby; this row of houses replaced two cottages and an orchard. During the 1920s-40s many of the houses were used as clubs for bridge, gambling and "congenial company". Ferry Road was known as Thames Street in the 1700s.

A photograph taken outside The Ringers shows HM King George VI and his brother, the Duke of Kent, walking in the funeral cortège for George Mountbatten, 2nd Marquis of Milford Haven on the 13th April 1938. The service had taken place at St Michael's Church where Bobby Howes sang in the choir and was therefore present at the funeral. The Marquis was to be buried in Bray Cemetery. He had lived at Lynden Manor in Holyport and his nephew, Prince Philip (later the Duke of Edinburgh) used to stay there during his school holidays. The Marquis' younger brother was Lord Louis Mountbatten of Burma.

9. War Memorial (II)

This stands on an area once known as **Holman's Mat** – an area of grassland with a large tree, and where mini-fairs were sometimes held. The Mat was reduced to its current size in order to widen the road when **Ferry End** was built. The **War Memorial** was dedicated in 1920 by the Bishop of Oxford with the names of villagers who died in the First World War; a further stone was added at the front following the Second World War. The commemorative rose bed was originally provided by the Women's Institute and is now maintained by Bray Parish Council. New rose bushes, called The Queen Elizabeth II Rose, were planted in 2022 to mark the Queen's Platinum (70th) Jubilee.

Holman's Mat

Next to the War Memorial can be seen the Honours Board which recognises Bray's involvement in the annual Britain in Bloom competition which is organised by the Royal Horticultural Society. Supported by local residents and businesses, Bray has always been extremely successful, both regionally and nationally, including Best Small Village in 2014. While Bray no longer enters the competition, volunteers continue to maintain the floral displays with financial support from Bray Parish Council.

There are several listed buildings along the High Street dating from the 15th and 16th centuries.

Ferry End with the War Memorial on the corner opposite

10. Thames House (II) (Bray Newsagents & Post Office); **Rickhams (II); The Old Dutch House (II); Stuart Cottage (II) and The Shottery (II)**

Look out for: The front doors and ground floors of the cottages are now below street level as layers of road surface have accumulated over a long period. Hundreds of years ago, the road through Bray up to the Lich Gate was laid with logs. Although covered over, it was only in 1970 that proper foundations were constructed.

At the beginning of the 1900s **Thames House** was a baker's shop, the 1901 Census describing the occupant Thomas Marks as Baker and Grocer. His son Frederick, was also a baker. In 1927 it was bought by the West Brothers who ran the local taxi and "Blue Bus Service" which ran until 1968. During the war period a large shed was built on the land behind and was used for assembling parts for tanks and airplanes. Latterly the site became a garage and is now a gated development of new houses called West Court. Those rooms which were not needed as showrooms have been used as a tobacconist & newsagents, a ladies' hairdresser owned by Miss Morris in the 1930s and a sub-post office. Coincidentally, for a short period during 2021-2022 it reverted to being a coffee shop,

The Old Post Office Bray, selling pastries and bread. There remains a small name-plate, saying Thames House, over the front door.

Rickhams has also been called Rickman, Thames Cottage and Rivernear. It is thought the rear of the house consists of an old Tudor cottage with a new front added in the 18th century although parts were destroyed in a fire at the end of World War II. The kitchen and room on the right (previously the garage) were built in the 19th century.

The **Old Dutch House** was once called "Dormer Cottage" and was a farmhouse with a pond. Its present name comes from a previous owner called Miss Holland whose nickname was "Old Dutch". The ground floor beams in **Stuart Cottage** and **The Shottery** suggest they were built around 1450 and are typical of foresters' cottages of that time.

Opposite The Shottery is **Bray Hair Studio**. Although rebuilt in 1935, a much earlier building was Jones' Shop. This was opened by Anne Jones in 1760, Dealer in Teas and Tobaccos. It remained in the same family for two hundred years, latterly also becoming the Sub-Post Office, before the Post Office section moved to the Corner Shop opposite and then to Thames House in the 1960s. Coincidentally, the 1901 Census names Anne Jones, widow, as Grocer & Post Mistress. By 1911, her son Albert Edward Jones had taken over as Grocer & Storekeeper, with his brother Thomas

Warner Jones described as Grocer & Sub-Postmaster, living at The Post Office, Bray on the corner of the Terrace, opposite. Freddie Jones, another member of the family, was also a bellringer.

The postal service must have been extremely efficient. In the 1887 Directory, it states that letters arrived at 7.10 am and 12.10 pm, and were dispatched at 12.10 and 6.50 pm. There was even a Sunday arrival & dispatch at 11.10 am. By 1899, there were three arrivals and dispatches per day, from both Maidenhead and Windsor plus one on Sundays.

11. The Crown Public House (II)

It is thought **The Crown** dates from 1335-1380 although this cannot be proved. The oldest part is the central section with the left and right-hand sections being two separate cottages; the right-hand cottage was a bicycle repair shop until it became part of the Inn in the early 20th century while the left-hand cottage remained a residence until 1955. It is known that it was a hostelry selling beer at the time of George II (1727-60) although legend has it that Charles II stopped off for a drink on his way to visit Nell Gwynn at Old Philiberts in Holyport, sixty years or so earlier. The Crown was granted a full licence in 1956.

An old newspaper article from the Maidenhead Advertiser, although sadly not dated, relates to a fire that took place in the part of the Crown known as the **Crown "Cot"**. Since it refers to the then tenant Mr W.T. Marks who had resided there since 1914, the fire must have been a few years later. Mr Marks had cycled into Maidenhead at about 11.00 am to do some shopping as his wife and children were away.

Mrs Portsmouth, the licensee of the inn, *"was in the kitchen at the back of the hotel peeling potatoes when she noticed dense smoke issuing from the upper part of the Cot"*. The place was well alight and the window panes cracking with the heat. Having raised the alarm, villagers *"were quickly on the scene and rendered splendid assistance in removing furniture from the inn as that part of the structure threatened to become involved"*.

Following *"a heroic effort to battle with the flames"* by the villagers, the **Bray Fire Brigade** arrived at ten minutes before midday. *"They immediately connected up the hose to the Cut, near by, and played on the fire which had got a fairly good hold on the back bedroom of the Cot"*. Having *"worked assiduously at their task"* while another squad *"worked liked trojans"* the fire was brought under control. When they were able to enter the Cot, *"it was then seen that the bedrooms and their contents at the rear were quite ruined; three spring mattress beds were burned almost beyond recognition and only the frames remained"*. A Valor Perfecta oil stove and an empty petrol tin were discovered.

When Mr Marks was later interviewed by an Advertiser representative, he explained he was not covered by insurance and *"admitted that he left the oil stove burning near the wood partition in one of the back bedrooms so as to keep the place aired, and with regard to the finding of the petrol tin he said he had about half a gallon of petrol in it which he used for the purposes of cleaning"*. Fortunately, the Brigade had prevented the fire spreading to the inn.

Continue along the High Street into Upper Bray Road and on to Jesus Hospital.

12. Jesus Hospital, including the Chaplain's House, Almshouses and Chapel (I)

Originally founded by **William Goddard** of the **Worshipful Company of Fishmongers**, Jesus Hospital was opened in 1628 for 40 poor people; it was taken over by the **Donnington Hospital Trust** in 2010. This is the oldest charity in Berkshire and was founded in 1393. There are now 20 residents.

Since it is private property, it is not possible to go inside the quadrangle although you can peer through the passageway from the pavement. The front gardens have been totally refurbished in a style in-keeping with the age of the building.

Thanks go to **Jim Jackson**, one of the previous Wardens, who wrote this short piece on the history of Jesus Hospital.

"*Jesus Hospital is considered by many to be "The Jewel in the crown of Bray" with I believe some justification. It was built between 1623-1627 with funds allocated by William Goddard, a very wealthy merchant with extensive land holdings in the area and others in London.*
"*Originally built to house the poorest members of the community in very basic accommodation, the properties are now modified and enlarged and provide desirable accommodation in a very pleasant setting and are generally reserved for senior people of "limited means" who have long term connections to the area.*
"*William Goddard died in 1609 and reputedly left instructions with his good friend Sir John Leman, who was Lord Mayor of London and a prominent member of The Worshipful Company of Fishmongers, not to begin the construction until his wife had died which was not until 1623.*
"*The red brick properties are arranged around a quadrangle with the "Chaplains House" (now the Wardens House) situated above the front entrance, and the Chapel at the far end of the footpath. This has a rather splendid stained-glass window, and what is probably an original Jacobean screen although not installed until the Victorian period; the adjoining garden is laid to lawns bordered by flowerbeds. Services are conducted in the chapel by The Vicar of Bray.*

"As you enter by the front door of Jesus Hospital there is a small museum on the right which houses a "Tavern Clock" also known as an "Act of Parliament Clock" which has almost certainly been on the premises since the end of the 18th Century and still keeps excellent time.

"There are also many items of interest including old keys and locks, silver badges required to be worn by the "inmates", Visitors Books containing autographs of many famous people including Prince Philip, the Duke of Edinburgh (17th December 1959 – he was Renter Warden for the Fishmongers' Company), Sir Edward Elgar, George Bernard Shaw, Dame Nellie Melba and, more recently, Theresa May MP and Sir Michael Parkinson.

"The properties stand in several acres of land with a "Spinney" surrounded by mature trees, bordered on the South by the "Cut", a drainage channel leading into the Thames.

"Jesus Hospital has a Communal room known as the "Reading Room" and sometimes as the "Victoria Room" which residents can use to relax or entertain and is generally used for communal activities. There is also a small "Guest Suite" that residents may use as accommodation for visiting friends or relatives.

"Jesus Hospital is an asset to the community being rather beautiful in its design and practical in its use.

"It is Grade One listed throughout and amongst the oldest buildings in Bray."

The Harbour of Refuge. (Walker.) Tate Gallery.

Pieces of old clay pipes were discovered under the windows when the front gardens at Jesus Hospital were replanted in 2012. One can imagine aged residents leaning out of their windows, smoking and dropping the disposable pipes on to the ground. These are in the little museum at Jesus Hospital and date from the 17th – 18th centuries. Similar pieces of old pipe are frequently found at the allotments – dropped and left by much later local folk, in the 19th and early 20th centuries.

Return to the Village Hall, the car park and allotments on land donated to Bray Parish Council by the Clothmongers' Guild in September 1980.

Building work started on **Bray Village Hall** in 1922 with an extension in 1924 to provide the bar and billiard area. A donation was made by William West Neve, an architect who lived in the nearby Fishery Estate. An opening night concert included the Australian singer, Dame Nellie Melba. Further subscriptions were raised from villagers.

The hall became the centre of village life with concerts – Bray even had its own orchestra, most of whom seem to have been members of the Howes family. Leonora, Bobby's aunt, played the piano; Edward, his uncle, played the violin; and Catherine, his mother, played the tambourine.

In 1923, a billiard table was donated by the industrialist, Sir Hugo Cunliffe-Owen who lived at Weir Bank, next to Monkey Island.

In 1940, the hall committee was asked to remove the billiard table so that lady volunteers could assemble magnetos (electrical generators) for Spitfires and Hurricanes. The table was carefully dismantled and carried on a wheelbarrow through the High Street to St Michael's Hall where it was stored until 1945. The names of those who moved the billiard table are written in chalk on the underside in commemoration. The only one which is decipherable is Robert Claude Howes ("Bobby" Howes). According to Bobby, two other men present were Johnny Molloy and John Norsworthy – the latter was verger at St Michael's for many years.

The billiard table has now been moved to a new home to make room for a wider range of social activities in the bar area.

The Home Guard also used the hall to practise their skills using wooden rifles and pitchforks.

An article in the Maidenhead Advertiser in June 2013, celebrating 90 years of the building, features Bobby Howes, the then Chairman of the Bray Village Hall Committee. He recalls his involvement with the hall since he was 16 when he was part of the Youth Club. Bobby also remembered Saturday nights in particular when American and Canadian troops, who were stationed in Bray during the Second World War, visited the hall and girls came to dance with them. Afterwards, the "Snowdrops", a derogatory term used to describe the American military police in their white helmets and gloves, came to take away the drunken soldiers.

As mentioned earlier, a boxing ring was built in the 1950s, subsequently being used as a stage. Bobby Howes recalls that there was a sprung floor where the boxing took place until, one day, he fell through it and it was replaced with the floor that is there today. Nowadays the hall remains a central feature of the village with a pre-school during the day and events in the evenings and weekends.

Look down Old Mill Lane with The Terrace to the right.

The Terrace is a row of brick cottages built in three stages and completed in 1900. No 1 started as a butcher's before becoming a grocer's shop. Later, it also acquired the Sub-Post Office counter. During the second half of the 20th century this was run as a delicatessen by Stan Bowler, although his father had first purchased the business in 1937. Stan was a Parish Councillor and acquired the title of "Mayor of Bray" – two brick plant containers were built in his memory down by the slipway.

Walk back towards the River, either along Ferry Road (turn down by the War Memorial) or continue along Old Mill Lane and turn left into Bettoney Vere. Here you will see six houses built on the site of an orchard in 1906 by Mr T.J. Digby.

13. Vicarage Cottage (II) & Linum Cottage (II)

The front of **Vicarage Cottage** was rendered in the 1920s at the same time as the right-hand wall was replaced; the original consisted of two 14th or 15th century half-timbered cottages covered in wattle and daub. They were occupied by foresters from Windsor Forest. The left-hand cottage was one up, one down whilst the right-hand cottage had two rooms on each floor plus a byre (cowshed). Apparently, there used to be a coffin hole in the ceiling of one of the downstairs rooms as the staircase was not big enough to allow a coffin to be taken up or down. The central chimney keeps the house upright! Although the earth floors were two feet below street level, they were not susceptible to flooding. There was a ghost who frequented the house up until 60 or so years ago, a White Lady - fortunately she was considered friendly.

The photograph below of **Linum Cottage** shows it when it was the original Waterside Inn. After the Inn moved to the other side of the road, this 18th century building was sold and became a private residence. The first house on the right is **Rose Cottage**.

It is worth walking down to the slipway and looking at the present-day Waterside Inn whilst recalling some of the river's previous history at this point.

The restaurant that is now **The Waterside Inn**, was originally a private house called Charlese before becoming the George Inn. William, an earlier member of the Woodhouse family mentioned previously, is shown as the Innkeeper of The George Inn in the Census Returns for 1851 followed by his eldest son William in 1861 & 1871. When William jnr died, his wife Eliza became the hotel keeper / licensed victualler at the Hinds Head with her daughters Sarah and Clara (1881 & 1891). The George became popular with visitors from London, becoming famous for "wine, women and song". Eventually the police took away the licence and it became once again a private house named Charlese.

In 1948, the brewery that owned the Waterside Inn (now Linum Cottage) bought Charlese and transferred their licence and premises across the road. **Michel and Albert Roux** bought the Waterside in 1972. In 1974, the Waterside Inn was awarded its first Michelin Star, followed by the second in 1977. In 1984 Albert took sole control of Le Gavroche in London and Michel took on The Waterside. The Waterside Inn was awarded three Michelin stars in 1985 and has retained the accolade to this day. Michel died in 2020 and the organisation is now run by his son, Alain, who is Chef Patron.

Bray was famous for eels and one resident has a painting of the river showing the "eel bucks" - baskets made of willow, used to catch fish along the Thames. A small weir with a channel made from branches with nine eel bucks attached. These bucks, made from woven willow, were lowered into the river during a particular season where eels would be caught in the basket.[8]

---

[8] Photograph "Eel traps on the Thames at Bray", dated 1885, courtesy of Historic England

The river was shallow at this point and people could even wade across when it was particularly low, a crossing that goes back hundreds of years and one of the possible reasons why the church is situated where it is. A ferry in the form of a punt ran regularly from Bray across to the towpath on the other side. Henry, another member of the Woodhouse family, is shown in the 1887 and 1899 Directories as running a steam launch, pleasure boat to Maidenhead as well as being a punt & canoe builder. Several people owned the boat yard, including E Howes.

It was bought by RH Messum in 1923 and, from 1946 to 1971, Geoffrey Messum ran the business including the hire of cruisers. The 1939 England & Wales Register describes Richard H Messum, Boat Builder & Licenced Waterman; his sons Gwyn R Messum, Electric & Marine Engineer & Waterman and Colin L Messum, Motor Boat Driver & Waterman. They all lived at The Ryepeck which is now owned by the Waterside Inn and is situated at the far end of their car park. Geoffrey G Messum is described as a Marine Engineer & Waterman, living at The Hutch. The wives of Richard Messum & Geoffrey Messum are both described as carrying out *"unpaid domestic duties"*.

looking across to the slipway and boat yard

HM Queen Elizabeth II landed at the slipway from the Windsor Regent on 18th October 1974 – a cold, wet and miserable day weather-wise – and walked as far as Bettoney Vere.

the Windsor Regent and Bray Slipway

SECTION 3 : OLD MILL LANE and MONKEY ISLAND

Old Mill Lane

Moving away from the centre of the Bray, continue down Old Mill Lane, past Bettoney Vere to where the road takes a sharp bend to the right. The road is named after the Mill and Mill House that were situated further along the Mill Stream. Originally it was called Monkey Island Road – now, the section beyond the Old Mill is called **Monkey Island Lane**. An island separates the Mill Stream from the main course of the river.

Along this stretch of the river was a Wharf and landing stage where coal and timber were unloaded. The 1848 Directory mentions Charles Mickley, describing him as a "Wharfinger", meaning "an owner or keeper of a wharf". The wharf is shown on the 1870-75 Ordnance Survey (OS) map. Further references in the 1851 Census and 1854 Directory, and subsequent Census returns and Directories, again refer to Charles Mickley, coal merchant. He owned the business for nearly 50 years until he died in October 1894, aged 83, and was buried in St Michael's churchyard.

The building that is now an Italian restaurant, **Caldesi in Compagna**, started life as a lodging for the bargees who delivered the coal. The 1870-75 OS map shows the **Albion PH** (public house). It continues as an inn with The Albion described in the 1901 Census with Stephen Brambley as the Beerhouse Keeper. It remained a pub for nearly all of the 20th century until it was eventually sold, the inside completely refurbished and it became The Fish restaurant. The Fish didn't last for too long, the next venture being a fusion restaurant. Finally, it was bought and continues to be run by **Giancarlo and Katie Caldesi**.

The large community of flats and townhouses called **Braybank** was built in 1964 on the site of another one of Bray's infamous hostelries, the **Hotel de Paris.** It was first built as a late Victorian mansion known as **Braymead** by Frederick Islay Pitman from Edinburgh. He lived there with his wife Helen and daughters for around 20 years and he is recorded in the Electoral Register of 1900. Apparently, Mr Pitman was also the official starter of the annual Oxford and Cambridge boat race. The 1911 Census shows that numerous staff were employed to look after the family and house with its 23 rooms, including 2 ladies maids and 2 table maids.

Since there is no mention of Mr Pitman in the 1920 Directory, he had presumably left Bray and a syndicate of local people got together to run the house as a hotel – **Braymead Court Hotel.** The venture proved unsuccessful and, in 1928, it was bought by the owners of the Café de Paris in London and became the Hotel de Paris. This time, the purchase was a success and became a centre for high life during the 1930s with the rooms *"much admired by members of London Society and the Stage; also by visitors from overseas"*. The hotel was used as the venue for Mr Ernest Simpson to be caught in the act of adultery so that his wife Wallis Simpson could achieve her divorce, prior to marrying Edward, Prince of Wales, later Duke of Windsor.

A local resident retains an original brochure from her parents-in-law who had connections with the hotel. Some of the descriptions are delightful asking guests (described above) to look at the brochure as a reminder *"of a pleasant rendezvous"*. Visitors were assured they *"will find contentment here, all year round."* The hotel had *"Perhaps the best known Ballroom outside the Metropolis. Soft light and sweet music bring mellow charm as you dance on a perfect floor"*. The *"beautiful grounds which covered an area of 6 acres, comprised of velvet lawns and studded with fine old trees and rare shrubs"*.

Hotel de Paris

The hotel never recaptured its allure after the Second World War and was finally closed and the land sold, making way for Braybank.

In Section 2, reference was made to Mr T.J. Rigby who built the rows of houses in Ferry End (opposite the War Memorial) and Bettoney Vere. He also built some of the houses along Brayfield Road as well as owning older properties in the Village. Mr Digby bought The Mill House from the son of William Eggleton who had worked as Miller and Farmer from at least 1876 with references in the 1891, 1901 and 1911 Census returns. Mr Eggleton owned much of the surrounding land which was also sold to Mr Digby. This land included what is now **River Gardens** – a site which had once contained a paper mill and, according to the 1870-75 OS map, an iron foundry (disused). Mr Digby subsequently sold all his properties and land to Newcombe Estates. In 1923 there was a large auction of the Bray Mill Estate held at the Braymead Court Hotel.

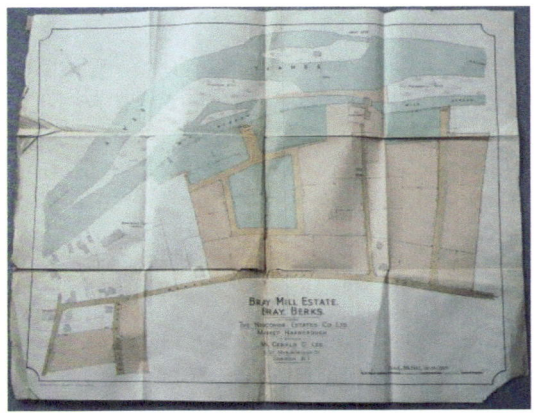

The sale included The Mill House and 40 houses ranging in value from £500 to £3000 *"all situated in the Beautiful Old-World Village of Bray"*. Also for sale were plots on the "Riverside Building Estate" which led to the Mill Stream and contained *"private landing stages, tennis courts, boating, bathing, fishing and golf"* – at least within driving distance. The map above is from the Auction catalogue.

At the end of the day, not a single house nor plot of land were sold. The houses were all occupied with the tenants on varying agreements of occupancy and the plans for the plots of land were considered locally as a case of "over-development". Eventually, the houses were sold individually and new houses gradually built in River Gardens. At the same time, houses were being built along Old Mill Lane as far as the motorway – although of course, it was not there during this period.

River Gardens runs alongside the Mill Stream with Headpile Eyot opposite. Old Mill Lane turns left, down to the Mill House although it has now been greatly altered. The road becomes Monkey Island Lane as it crosses the M4 motorway. A new bridge was installed in 2020 as the motorway was widened to become a "Smart Motorway". In the process of surveying the old bridge, it was discovered the structure was suffering from "concrete cancer" so the new work was timely.

Around Monkey Island

Once over the motorway you will see a driveway with the sign **Weir Bank**. The original house was built and lived in by Mr Digby. Later it was owned by **Sir Hugo-Cunliffe Owen**, who donated the billiard table to the Village Hall and, who used the land on both sides of the road as a stud farm. His most famous horse was Felstead, who won the 1928 Derby. Nowadays, it has been turned into several offices run by Bray Business Centre.

At the end of the tarmacked road, you can turn left into **Monkey Island Estate**. The buildings that make up Monkey Island Estate are built on an **"eyot"** – pronounced "ait" as in the number 8. There are several eyots in this stretch of the Thames, being an old English word meaning a small island in a river, especially the River Thames. Mention has been made of the eyot opposite River Gardens, with Pigeonhill Eyot after the Mill House. Queen's Eyot near Bray Marina is owned by Eton College.

Queen's Eyot

Next to the hotel car park is an eighteenth century white timber framed house called **Long White Cloud** although, up until the 1920s at least, it was named **The Hut.** It has now been luxuriously restored and redecorated by Monkey Island Estate for use as private lets.

It has had several illustrious owners in its past including **Miss Van de Weyer, a lady-in-waiting to Queen Victoria**. Reputedly, the Queen used to call in for tea on occasions when she was staying at Windsor Castle. A telegram would be sent to the Sub-Post Office in Bray informing Miss Van de Weyer of the Queen's intended visit. A runner carried the telegram down the lane to warn of the imminent arrival, so that it was not a surprise!

Long White Cloud

Sir Edward Elgar was a friend of Leo Francis "Frank" Schuster, a patron of the arts, who owned The Hut from the late 1800s until he died in 1927 (reference the 1899, 1915 and 1920 Directories). Elgar composed several of his works whilst staying there and concerts were held in the Music Room, overlooking the Thames. Other visitors included the Australian operatic soprano, Dame Nellie Melba, musician Gabriel Fauré, conductor Sir Adrian Boult, war poet Siegfried Sassoon and playwright George Bernard Shaw. Both Sir Edward Elgar and Dame Nellie Melba signed the visitors' book at Jesus Hospital.

The Land of the Long White Cloud was a Maori name given to New Zealand when they arrived in the country by canoe. There are two theories on how "The Hut" was rechristened "Long White Cloud". It is suggested that Frank Schuster enlarged and renamed the house in recognition of a friend, Captain Leslie Wylde who was born in New Zealand and his new wife, artist Wendela Boreel. Another suggestion is that the family of Stirling Moss renamed it when they lived there. Since their previous house in Tring was called White Cloud Farm, this is a possibility. Leslie Wylde and Wendela Boreel inherited the house from Frank Schuster when he died. Wylde died in 1935 and the house was sold.

Sir Stirling Craufurd Moss, a Formula One racing driver, spent part of his youth growing up at Long White Cloud with his parents Alfred and Aileen, and his sister Pat who became a successful rally driver as well as a very good horse rider. In fact, both his parents were also keen on motorsports with his father racing at Brooklands. At the age of seven, Stirling Moss was given an old Austin Seven which he would drive around the fields near his home. Apparently, he also raced up down the nearby Drift Road in a Mini-Cooper. Stirling Moss participated in British Motor Sports, including Formula One, from 1948 – 1962 when he retired from the sport following a serious accident.

A photo display in the entrance hall of the house explains that he won 212 of the 529 races he entered across several categories, including winning 16 Formula One Grand Prix races. He died aged 90 in April 2020.

A pedestrian bridge straddles the Mill Stream taking you across to the main hotel buildings although the idea of a bridge is a relatively new addition as previously one could only reach the island by boat. It is worth pausing to look at the buildings, both of which contain parts which are Grade 1 listed – **the Pavilion** on the left and **the Temple** on the right.

This time there are three theories on how the island acquired its name. The first, believed to be the most likely, is that the island belonged to the Canonesses of Burnham Abbey, the island taking on the name "Bournhames Eyte" during the Middle Ages. There could have been a monastic connection, with the name deriving from "monks". An alternative theory is linked to the frieze of monkeys mimicking human behaviour which can be seen in the room below the Pavilion's octagonal upper chamber. Finally, the Spencers managed the fishing around the island during most of the 18th century. Fisherman would come to the island and pay to fish. A colloquial name for money was "monkey", leading to the name Monkey Island – where you came to pay to fish.

The Fire of London in 1666 caused a great deal of devastation and much of the City needed to be rebuilt. Barges of Oxfordshire stone were taken into London, returning with loads of rubble from the construction sites which were dumped on several of the islands in the Thames, including "Burnham-Ayt". This established a solid base, lifting the land above flood height. **Monkey Island Hotel** was first built around 1735-8 as a fishing pavilion and banqueting house for **Charles Spencer, 3rd Duke of Marlborough**, who had bought the island in 1723.[9]

---

[9] A History of Monkey Island Estate published by YTL Hotels.

Two dates are given for when Charles Spencer bought Monkey Island – 1723 and 1738. I have used the date given in the Estate's own guide. There is a letter, dated September 1738, written by Frances Countess of Hartford to Henrietta Countess of Pomfret, in which she says: "I went last week to see a little island, which the Duke of Marlborough has bought, at Bray, and which, with the decorations is said to have cost him eight thousand pounds." She goes on to describe the house and the ceiling painted with monkeys. Since the Duke appears to have commissioned the Pavilion with "singerie" and the Temple, the earlier date would appear to be correct as it is highly unlikely that he would have had all the work carried out and completed in less than nine months. The island is named "Duke of Marlborough Island" on the John Roque map mentioned previously.

As mentioned above, the ceiling and upper walls of the ground floor room in the Pavilion are painted with monkeys dressed in clothes and acting out human summer pursuits, such as fishing, punting and shooting, in a style known as **"singerie"**. The paintings and raised gilded borders have now been beautifully restored and can be seen as one walks through to the bar and bistro restaurant. By 1792, the island had become known as "Monkey Island".

Over the next few decades, the island acquired new owners and by 1840 the Pavilion had become a riverside inn reached by a ferry and observed by people enjoying leisure trips on the Thames. The 1871, 1881 and 1891 Census returns show Robert Plummer as Hotel Keeper and Licensed Victualler. According to accounts in A History of Monkey Island Estate, Mrs Plummer was serving meals on the lawn and drinks through the window of the bar next to the Monkey Room. The venue proved to be particularly popular with boys from Eton College. Thanks to Mrs Plummer, the Hotel established a reputation for *"decent dining"* serving eels, perch and jack freshly caught in the stream.

By the early 1900s, Monkey Island attracted the attention of Edward VII and Queen Alexandra with a photograph from 1905 showing them *"taking tea"* on the lawn with other members of their family and entourage.

In 1959, the island was bought by Christopher "Kit" Reynolds for his mother, Lady Reynolds, upon her return from India. He set about restoring and expanding the facilities so that in the 1960s and 70s it had become the new social centre in Bray with music, dancing, dining and general fun. Monkey Island wasn't just open to

47

members of high society; locals could also enjoy a light lunch or tea on the lawn.

Sadly, this did not continue and for the next 30 or so years, the ownership changed hands several times. Its reputation went steadily downhill and the buildings took on an air of neglect. In May 2015, Tan Sri Yeoh Tiong Lay, the Malaysian Chairman of the YTL Corporation, discovered the island and wanted to "resurrect" the Hotel and grandeur of the island. It was a much smaller hotel than the others owned by the company but finally his sons took on the project in his memory, following their father's death in 2017. It proved to be an enormous undertaking but the end result is there for all to see, including a statue of their father in a large chair sitting under a tree.

Hopefully you have enjoyed your stroll around the village. The final two sections provide an overview for those who have an interest in the natural environment and archaeology.

SECTION 4 : NATURAL BRAY

Bray is surrounded for the most part by Green Belt, an area of land which encircles virtually the whole of London. The concept of a *"green girdle"* was first initiated in 1929 to compensate for the *"deficiency of green spaces in the capital"*. It came to also represent the prevention of developments spreading further and further into the countryside. This area of farmland and fields is in theory protected by law but the need for housing is putting a great deal of pressure on Authorities to overcome the regulations and develop new sites. Bray Parish Council works hard to protect the Green Belt.

Reference has already been made to the River Thames which borders one side of the village. Old paintings show pictures of the eel baskets that used to lie across the river, a tradition that died out a long time ago. Nowadays, the river is used purely by pleasure craft. Otters have returned to the Thames and have been seen locally although they tend to be nocturnal animals and, should you think you've spotted one during the day, it is more likely to be a mink. These will have escaped from a farm and are now considered a pest owing to the damage they cause.

If you are lucky, you may see the turquoise blue and orange flash of a kingfisher. More common are the mute swans, royal birds owned and protected by the King or Queen and two livery companies. Historically, this was to ensure there was a sufficient supply of this luxury meat for royal banquets and feasts. Every July, the ceremony of **Royal Swan Upping** takes place led by the Queen's Royal Swan Marker, with his white swan's feather in his cap, and Royal Swan Uppers together with Swan Uppers from The Worshipful Company of Vintners and the Worshipful Company of Dyers.

They row along the Thames from Sunbury near Hampton Court to Abingdon in Oxfordshire, catching the year's cygnets and ringing them to show ownership while checking their health. Swans are no longer eaten and killing them may be charged as illegal but numbers are still counted every year, monitoring the population. In recent years, a pair of swans has nested on Bray slipway, keeping all intruders well at bay. Don't try to approach them, especially after the cygnets have hatched.

Cormorants perch on the posts in winter, drying their wings and catching fish, much to the annoyance of local fishermen who claim the birds are taking too many! Great crested grebe, Canada, Egyptian and greylag geese are all regular visitors. In summer, swifts, swallows and house martins swoop over the water catching flies.

the Cut in winter

The Cut feeds into the Thames. The stretch alongside Bray is full of silt and fallen branches although there is a plan to clear the waterway so that small boats can travel from Maidenhead. In 2013 the Environment Agency built a weir near The Causeway to encourage fish to breed. Coots, moorhens, mallards, yellow wagtails and herons live within the vicinity, with teal in winter.

You cannot walk along the Thames on this side of the river. You need to cross to the Buckinghamshire bank. If you would like a longer walk, you can visit Bray Lock, first built in 1845, with the current lock built in 1888. The river was difficult for barges and small boats to navigate at this point, being fast flowing with many shallow areas. Apparently, the lock gates were kept open after heavy rain fall when water levels were high and only used when water levels were low, to allow deeper channels for river craft. The mill owner was allowed to charge a toll.

Bray Lock looking downstream

To reach Bray Lock, walk down Old Mill Lane into Monkey Island Lane, past the gates across the road, the water works and soon you will see a cycleway sign and footpath to your left. At the end of this path is the Summerleaze footbridge, put in place by the local gravel company whose depot is further along on the right. As you cross the bridge (warning it can be slippery in winter) Bray Lock is upstream to the left, and Bray Marina, downstream to the right. Referring to Section 5, the marina is the possible site of Hoveringham Pit. When on the bridge, look in the direction of 2 o'clock, and you may be able to see Windsor Castle in the distance.

You can also spot the two Dorney Rowing Lakes, owned by Eton College, and used for the rowing events in the 2012 London Olympics.

Having crossed the bridge, turn left along the tow path towards Bray Lock and Maidenhead. You will see the river view of Monkey Island Estate. Spend some time watching boats come in and out of the lock, especially when it is busy at weekends during the summer. Nowadays, the locks are all automated at the push of a button; gone are the days when one had to push or pull the heavy wooden "arms" in order to open or close the gates.

It is worth walking past Bray Lock a short way until you are opposite Bray slipway where you can see The Waterside Inn and St Michael's Church. Allow 1½ hours if you do this walk from and back to Bray. If you want a longer walk, you can continue along the tow path to Maidenhead or turn right at the bridge and it is about 5 miles (8kms) to walk alongside the river to Eton and into Windsor. Warning: the tow path can be muddy in winter and after heavy rain.

In days gone by, parts of Bray would have flooded, the last serious flood being in 1947 when large sections of Windsor and Maidenhead were under water. In 2002, a Flood Relief Channel was opened parallel to the Thames, named **The Jubilee River**. This allows water to be diverted from Maidenhead, Bray, Eton and Windsor.

Another pleasant walk is to continue a little further along Monkey Island Lane, over the Cut with its metal railings, and immediately turn right towards Bray Lake. Again, an ex-gravel pit which is now used for various water sports. On the far side, you will see the new Thames Hospice which was opened in October 2020. You can walk round the lake and in the late Spring you can hear, and perhaps see, several different warblers amongst the reeds, as well as more common water birds on the lake itself. This path can also be very muddy, especially in winter, but worth doing if you have the right footwear.

Looking overhead you may well see red kites circling. Conservationists began a programme to reintroduce red kites into the Chiltern Hills in July 1990 where they bred successfully, spreading into neighbouring counties. One pair, breeds in trees next to the Bray allotments and their high-pitched mewing has become a familiar sound. You may hear the drumming of great spotted and green woodpeckers along with the husky call of pheasants.

At dusk, bats leave their hideaways in the church tower and under the tiles of the older houses. They are probably pipistrelles, another protected species. Tawny owls also live around the churchyard and can be heard calling to each other at night. Grey squirrels, foxes, muntjac and roe deer with the occasional badger and hedgehog complete the local wildlife.

SECTION 5 : EARLY HISTORY

Background
There are at least two theories on how "Bray" acquired its name. One thought is that it derives from "Bibroces", an ancient British tribe who resided in the local area. Another suggestion is that the word comes from the Gallic (French) word "Braium" meaning "marsh" or "wet place". Whilst Bray (spelt Brai) is mentioned in the Domesday Book[10] of 1086, there is evidence of much earlier settlement within the area dating back, in some cases, to prehistoric times.

Prehistoric Periods
The fact that Bray is situated alongside the River Thames means that the low-lying Thames Valley was a major source of food, movement of people and therefore settlement. Many of the artefacts, such as hand axes, flint and later shards of pottery, from the Stone, Bronze and Iron Ages were recovered during the excavation of gravel pits in the 19th and 20th centuries, from scattered remains found whilst field walking or more recently, through developer-funded excavations.

> *Stone, Bronze and Iron ages are terms used to describe more specific pre-historic periods and, as a generalisation, relate to the materials used to make implements and tools such as hand axes.*
> *Stone Age, to include:*
> *Palaeolithic = 500,000 – 10,000 BC*
> *Mesolithic = 10,000 – 4,000 BC*
> *Neolithic = 4,000 – 2,200 BC*
> *Bronze Age: 2,200 – 700 BC*
> *Iron Age: 700 BC – AD 43*

---

[10] The Domesday Book is the oldest surviving public record and is a highly detailed survey and valuation of land holding and resources covering much of England. It was commissioned by William the Conqueror in 1085 following his Conquest in 1066 so he could find out who owned what, how much it was worth and how much was owed to him as King in tax, rents and military service. The Domesday Book, as it became known, was published in manuscript form in 1086.

There are however question marks relating to where sites excavated over one hundred years ago were actually situated in relation to modern buildings, alongside the fact that the recording of any findings was not as rigorous as it is today.

During the time when extraction for gravel was carried out by hand, it was possible to monitor the pits and search the spoil heaps. All the lakes you see around Bray are the result of gravel extraction which have been filled in to create wildlife areas or leisure facilities eg Bray Lake. Geological or land movement, changes in climate and human disturbance make it difficult to identify specific sites, except to provide evidence that man existed within the vicinity. One such example of a possible Palaeolithic site is at the Bray Triangle where there is a gravel pit that is on the left of the Upper Bray Road, past the Bailey Bridge, as you drive out of the village towards the A308.

On the outskirts of Bray village but within the Parish, lies a known Mesolithic site to the left of the A308(M) as you drive up to the M4 junction 8/9. This is now classified by Historic England as a Scheduled Monument. Flint scatters, including finished objects and manufacturing waste, have been excavated from this site. It is thought the site was occupied around 6,500-7000 BC. Another possible Mesolithic site is at Hoveringham Pit, probably where Bray Marina is now situated on the Windsor Road A308 side of Monkey Island Lane.

Man-made features start to emerge during the Neolithic period. These can be seen around the area with signs of occupation at Weir Bank Stud Farm (now gravel pits on the opposite side of Monkey Island Lane to Weir Bank) and Bray Triangle including Bronze Age pottery, postholes and a wooden post used in building structures such as a round house, pits and ditches. A few human remains have been excavated from Hoveringham Pit – a couple of skull fragments and part of a broken femur or thigh bone found close to a Neolithic antler comb and pottery fragments, and a partial skull found in the Thames at Monkey Island.

As we move into the Bronze Age, clearly definable settlements and agricultural field systems can be identified around Bray as shown in this extract from the East Berkshire report.[11]

"The densest settlement is recorded on the Thames river gravels at Bray, where a major site has been excavated at Weir Bank Stud Farm. Structures from the site include a roundhouse with associated occupation layers, and a four-post structure, possibly a granary. A number of other pits, hollows and post holes were also found along with artefact scatters and environmental remains. The site was enclosed by ditches and fences, which defined square 'co-axial' fields[12] and activity area. .... Nearby, at Bray Triangle, a number of pits and postholes may represent further circular Late Neolithic or Bronze Age structures."

The field systems at Weir Bank Stud Farm point to animals being kept there rather than cereal cultivation although charred plant remains indicate that this was also taking place. Further studies suggest that, by the Late Bronze Age, field systems within the Thames Valley area were centred on specific settlements. In this instance, Weir Bank Stud Farm was on the western edge of a group of settlements extending eastwards and centred around Runnymede. Bray was therefore part of a boundary zone with a different settlement group based to the west of Maidenhead. A few features, such as a pit, hollow and hearth were unearthed at Weir Bank Stud Farm and a dense scatter of pottery and animal bone were found at Hoveringham Pit. Mapping and studying these

---

[11] "Archaeology in East Berkshire: A Resource Assessment", a Report compiled for the Ardeola Charitable Trust by Dr Owen Humphreys, first published in January 2019.

[12] Co-axial field systems are one of several methods of land division employed during the Bronze Age. They generally consist of linear stone banks forming parallel boundaries running up slope to meet similar boundaries that run along the contours of higher slopes. The long strips formed by the parallel boundaries may be subdivided by cross banks to form a series of rectangular field plots, each sharing a common axis. Hut circle settlements, and funeral and ceremonial sites, may be found within these enclosed fields.

settlements start to show how humans were having an impact on the landscape.

Although the number of artefacts recovered from the area is fairly limited, the most significant finds have mainly been from the River Thames, including large amounts of metalwork deposited possibly as part of ritual practices. Two hoards, or deposits of valuable objects, have been found in Bray with another collection of objects found at Hoveringham Pit.

Overall, only a limited amount of evidence of Iron Age occupation has been discovered within the area. This may mean that sites have yet to be identified or that the area was marginal being on the edge of a larger cultural settlement to the east, as described above.

ROMAN (AD 43-410)
There are no urban or military sites in the East of Berkshire suggesting this was a rural landscape with ritual and industrial features alongside agricultural. Whilst there is evidence of substantial Roman settlement in the Bray riverside area further exploration is needed to fully understand the extent of any settlement. A mixed cremation and burial cemetery, with human remains dating to the 4th-5th centuries, has been excavated at Hoveringham Pit with sufficient building materials eg tiles, to suggest a villa. It should be noted that by referring only to sites specific to Bray, other Roman sites and potential settlements in East Berkshire are being ignored in this particular article.

Also linked to this period is a jetty excavated at Hoveringham Pit and the possible evidence of bridge piers (or pile dwellings) at Bray Lock suggesting the river formed part of the Roman infrastructure for the area. In addition, an axe has been found in the Thames at Bray.

EARLY MEDIEVAL (AD 410-1066)
To put this period into a more familiar context, the Romans for the most part had left Britain and the country was divided into separate kingdoms with urban settlements becoming an

established feature by the 10th and 11th centuries. Our knowledge is no longer based just on archaeological evidence but documentary records are starting to emerge in the form of chronicles and maps. The Angles, Saxons and Jutes (Anglo-Saxons) arrived from northern mainland Europe in the 5th and 6th centuries followed by the Danes (later to be known as the Vikings) from Scandinavian countries at the end of the 8th century. Kings Alfred, Guthrum, Aethelred the Unready and Cnut, to name but a few, reflect the changes and how the two enemies gradually merged to unite the country. Christianity also became established during this period.

Whilst later documentary evidence suggests there were established settlements around Bray there is little evidence on the ground other than a 5th century metalworking site at Hoveringham Pit. A church was built near Bray at some point during this period although there is no surviving structural evidence. If you look on the outside south wall near one of the doors on St Michael's Church Hall, embedded is an old stone with the carving of an animal, possibly a leashed hound or dog, which is thought may have come from the original Saxon church.

The Thames was a major transport route and monasteries housing small local communities developed along its banks. Permission has been granted for a major excavation to take place in the Paddock next to Holy Trinity Church in Cookham. In 2021, clear archaeological evidence was discovered to prove that a monastery or Minster was based there during the 8th and 9th centuries. The dig, which is overseen by Dr Gabor Thomas from the University of Reading, will take place for 4 weeks each summer from 2022-2024. This site is of national, and even international, importance in helping archaeologists and historians understand more about this period of Medieval history.

Outside the village, at Braywick Park, developer-funded excavations were carried out in the summer of 2018 on the site that now occupies Maidenhead's new Leisure and Sports Centre. Post holes were excavated indicating an Early Saxon settlement of at least six sunken buildings known as Pit Houses or Grub Huts.

SECTION 6 : ACKNOWLEDGEMENTS

The following leaflets and books have been used in putting together this short history, if you are interested in finding out more about the history of Bray:

- Bray Today and Yesterday by Nan Birney, edited by Richard Russell

- The Royal Hundred of Bray by Luke Over and Chris Tyrrell

- Church pamphlets, with thanks to John Seymour

- Paul Seddon, for advice, encouragement and permission to use the Berkshire Research paper; he was one of the founders of the project. I have used only the information relating to the area immediately surrounding Bray Village although the study extends beyond into East Berkshire.

- Elias Kupfermann, archaeologist and historian, for allowing me to use a section of the Windsor Garrison accounts and proof reading the final version

- Liz Cooper, whose original paintings I have used from the Royal Heritage of Bray map which celebrated the Queen's 60th Diamond Jubilee in 2012.

- Geoff Hayes, for his useful booklet on the Parish Fire Engine

- Andrew Jordan, Executive Vice-President, YTL Hotels & Properties UK for meeting with me and allowing me to use information from A History of Monkey Island Estate.

- Geoff Allison, for allowing me to scan his collection of old post cards.

- Robert "Bobby" Howes, one of Bray's oldest residents – the source of a range of local stories.

- Sandra Kiely, who carried out all the research on the names on the War Memorial and whose information I used for William Woodhouse.

- Margaret Pierce, for her background on the Woodhouse family.

- Paul Tillion, another of Bray's long-term residents who also provided local background.

- Jane Westerman, for her brochure on the Hotel de Paris and other information.